THE AT RISK CHILD

David Butler

ISBN: 1540770494
ISBN 13: 9781540770493
Library of Congress Control Number: 2016920202
CreateSpace Independent Publishing Platform
North Charleston, South Carolina

This is dedicated to my mother who gave birth to my two brothers and me. She left this world at the very young age of thirty-one. There are no photographs of her, and being so young when she passed, I only have images of her in my mind. I have always felt that she lives within me and watches over me.

TABLE OF CONTENTS

PREFACE

Have you ever wondered if a decision you made years ago, months ago, or even days ago was the right decision? Do circumstances in life limit our choices or give us opportunities for growth and self-actualization? Can our thoughts transcend our physical surroundings and bring us the life we have dreamed about?

Well I have. I have asked myself these questions throughout my life, first as a boy, as a newly promoted supervisor, and as VP and president of several companies. Time and experience have given me answers to many of life's questions. However, with these answers came a new question, "How do I pass along my knowledge to others?" The answer came years ago when I was offered the opportunity to give a presentation to students at a local college. That experience energized me and provided me a path I still follow today: speaking to young people.

A few years ago, I started to recall the challenges I faced throughout my life and how I learned to overcome them. I now share them with you. My hope is that you find, in the pages of this book, answers to some of the above questions.

David Butler

INTRODUCTION

The Beginning

I am eight years old, and I am sitting in the front row of benches in a very small Baptist church in New Orleans, Louisiana. The year is 1958, and things are quite different than they are now. No, that's an understatement. The living conditions are light-years from what they are today—no running water at home, wood-burning stoves, block ice for refrigeration, and no television. More on this later.

My mother is at rest in her coffin after losing a horrible battle with kidney disease. Mom had been fighting the illness as far back as I can remember. She suffered tremendous pain with no pathway to getting better. Dialysis, still not widely used, was not an option back then. She is only thirty-one years old and dead. I am sitting with my two brothers: one two years younger and the other two years older. The church choir is going through a litany of very sad old hymns. I could feel pain and unbelievable grief all around me. Just about everyone in the church is in tears, and some are crying very loudly. I then heard a lady say out loud, "Those three children have no mother, and now they are not going to make it in life." I began to wonder what would happen to me and my brothers. I remember those words as though they were spoken yesterday, and I remember thinking, "Why would we not make it? What would stop us?"

This book is a chronicle of my life and the sixty-plus years of facing adversity and thriving. It is my fervent hope that it provides some insight and inspiration to others who may be facing seemingly insurmountable challenges and problems in their lives. This isn't a "feel good" story that stands alone but more of a guide for living and achieving your fullest potential even when you have no idea what that might be. I have come to realize that life is truly a journey, and every day is a gift to be cherished and embraced. There is no single destination in life. We as human beings are imbued with the gift of constant growth and development, if we want it.

As I share the time line of my life and impart the critical-decision points that steered me to become who I am, you will see patterns emerge that show how blessed I have been and how I have shared my experiences and leadership with others over the years. You will see how seemingly small or seemingly insignificant decisions turn into major life-altering events. All the events that I describe happened to me. I will describe my movements and decisions through time and what their end results were. You will see the power of consistency of purpose and positive belief. My background could not have been any harsher or more meager, but those struggles have given me great strength to live life to the fullest. The sum of those experiences equipped me to become who I am in mind, body, and spirit.

Keep a journal. Keeping a journal of your life's events and day-to-day occurrences is important and allows you to see your own growth and development. This process works, and although it may seem uncomfortable in the beginning, you need to do it! I do!

CHAPTER 1

BORN WITH A VEIL

My family had been living and working on Stanton Plantation since the late 1800s. When my maternal grandfather died, his side of the family claimed his body for burial. To this day no one in our family knows where he is buried. With the death of my grandfather, my family, which included an extended family of aunts and uncles, was removed from the plantation and relocated to what was to become Lower Coast Algiers. The densely wooded and swampy community consisted of one street. Although we only had one paved street, there were many paths cut through the woods that led to other family members' houses. Our small community consisted of about thirty-five people.

Even before we moved from the plantation, details about my birth were known to all the families. This unusual birth, being born with a veil, led me to be looked at differently by all who knew. Some relatives looked at me with reverence and respect, some with fear and confusion. I looked at it as just who I was. The things that made me unique or viewed differently didn't bother me in the least. Each day of life that we are given is meant to be lived to the fullest by learning, working, and respecting everything about this planet.

What this means:
A veil is a mask covering the face of a child at birth. Such births are rare and hold special significance for the child born in this manner. In some cultures, this rare occurrence, roughly one in eighty thousand, is also known as being born behind the Veil. Those born behind the Veil are often found to have special abilities, such as finding underground water supplies, knowing when weather patterns will change, or predicting when fish and other food supplies will become plentiful. In ancient times they were held in high esteem for their knowledge in a wide range of disciplines, and therefore became known as great teachers. The Veil is sometimes also referred to as "The Veil of Tears." Due to ignorance or misunderstanding, these gifted people have been attacked or even killed. During dark times their abilities were thought to be that of witches. I was told by my maternal grandmother and aunts as early as I can remember (about three years old) that I was born with the gift of "second sight," a veil.

Throughout reading the story of my life and activities, you will see where this gift has manifested itself. Some famous people said to be born with a veil include:

Liberace—American musician and entertainer
James Couzens—Industrialist, banker, and politician
Queen Christina of Sweden
Frank Albert Jones—Black artist
Sigmund Freud—Austrian neurologist and father of psychoanalysis

Napoleon Bonaparte—Emperor of France
Lord Byron—English poet
Charlemagne—King of the Franks and founder of modern France and Germany
Albert Einstein—Theoretical physicist

CHAPTER 2

CARRYING WATER

One of my earliest memories as a young child growing up in Lower Coast Algiers was that there were always physical and mental challenges to overcome. One of the most precious commodities that was always in short supply was clean drinking, cooking, and bathing water. There was no running water in any of the houses in my small neighborhood. There was, however, one water hydrant that supplied fresh water to the entire area, which was located about three-quarters of a mile from our house. To retrieve the water, we would walk carrying gallon buckets with handles made of wire. I am about six years old, and I am struggling to carry the heavy, filled to the top, bucket back to the house. I can still remember how that handle would make a painful indentation in my tiny hands. Every few seconds I would have to change hands to alleviate the pain but being able to carry the water home was like a rite of passage and one of personal pride.

Although the journey, in all types of weather, seemed difficult at times, the water from the hydrant was a lot better tasting than the rain water that we used to capture draining off the tar roof tops. Collected rain water would often contain mosquito larvae which formed on the surface especially during the hot summers of Louisiana. We would be so thirsty that we would just brush everything aside, close our eyes, and drink. If it was night and the buckets were empty, we would make the long trip again to the single source of water supply. The thought never occurred to me that this was a terrible hardship and something crude and inhuman. I knew if the bucket was empty someone in our household had to make the walk. I was happy to be able to carry the bucket.

Another early memory was the use of a wood-burning stove for both heating and cooking. During the summer months, we needed wood for cooking purposes. However, during the long cold winters we had to constantly keep the stove going most of the day and throughout the night. When the stack of wood got low, we would venture outside even in the darkest nights to forage for dead tree limbs.

Once again this didn't seem harsh; it was just the reality of our existence. These little challenges were giving me the strength of mind and body to effectively handle many forthcoming life-altering challenges. At the time I didn't realize, not until much later, that this would be a theme which would run throughout my life.

Everyone who has ever lived has had to face challenges, be they rich or poor. How we handle these situations depends so much on the reservoir of strength and will that we build into ourselves through learning and enduring experiences. I have witnessed many people collapse physically and mentally in the face of duress. It doesn't have to be that way. Practice making your mind and body stronger every day, and the benefits will carry you forward for a very long, healthful time.

CHAPTER 3

PRONOUNCING MASSACHUSETTS

It is so very interesting and fateful how one word, "Massachusetts," or one situation can impact someone's future for years to come. How that one word helped me many years later in life to develop an extensive vocabulary and to become a better speaker when communicating with groups I supervised and worked with? In kindergarten, as a five-year-old, I never really had the occasion to speak many words. My mother and father never went to school and couldn't read or write. There were no books in the house to read, radio to listen to, or television to watch. I overheard my kindergarten teacher talking to the school principal about holding me back for a year. They hadn't really discussed the need to hold someone back before. As a result of that conversation, I was tested for various skills such as musical and reading ability. The musical aptitude landed me in a newly created violin class.

The following year the first graders were tested for our speech and pronunciation abilities by a language specialist from the school board. We were lined up alphabetically by last name. The first kids in front of me had words to pronounce such as pot, tree, and pencil. I relaxed when I heard these familiar easy words. My turn now. The word chosen for me was “Massachusetts.” Massachusetts! I panicked. As a six-year-old I had never heard the word before, and it had so many syllables. I went, “Massa, Massa, Massa,” and could not go any further. The special education teacher cast a critical frown at me and quickly scribbled some notes on her writing pad. I received my first label in school, “Stutterer.” I was immediately put into speech therapy that lasted the entire six years of elementary school. The extra class taught vocabulary once a week and reading skills once a week. In that sense, I enjoyed the experience. It would be years later, taking the preliminary scholastic aptitude test, SAT, and other types of diagnostic tests that I would discover I had a really well-developed vocabulary. It came automatically from all the reading and training I had experienced. What looked like another challenge, another something to push through, turned out to be a blessing. I have found that it just happens over and over again in my life, as well as in the lives of others. Adversity is merely a challenge, merely a set of circumstances, that allows us to flex our muscles of alternatives and figure out how to problem solve.

The week following our verbal testing, I met with our school board-appointed speech teacher. He was a very large man who never smiled and always looked pissed off about something. He always carried with him a very large brown duffel bag-type briefcase which held a huge wooden paddle. There were about eight of us, special needs kids, in his class. After the very first class, he gave us homework to complete and turn in the following week. Somehow, I got it done. Thank God for books with pictures above the words. One of the kids didn’t have his homework completed. He was from a well-known family in the community, but he definitely had some learning disabilities. The teacher called him up to the desk and told him to lean over it. The man removed the wooden paddle and proceeded to hit the boy with what seemed like all of his strength. The child started to cry silently; however, it didn't matter to this sadist. Every week the same beatings were repeated to anyone without completed homework. After a few weeks of this I made friends with my classmates and helped several with their homework. I don't know if corporal punishment was approved at that point in time but it was administered. Protecting the other students in class was something I just felt compelled to do. It's interesting that throughout my forty-five-year work life, I have continued to carry that same theme: I protect my co-workers, my employees, and my company.

At the end of the first grade, my teacher was bringing other teachers from the third, fourth and fifth grades to listen to me read. After the second grade, they were bringing me to their classes to work math problems. I thought all of this was par for the course. My father made me give up the violin because he thought it was a sissy instrument. I think the real reason was that he couldn't afford to buy me one to practice with and own.

As the years passed, being labeled "special" and a "stutterer" was now seen as a benefit by me. However, I had no idea what a blessing this would turn out to be in later years of my academic and work life.

Increasing your vocabulary is one of the best things you can do. You can carry a three-dollar dictionary around with you and literally pick up a word or two a day or use your smartphone to define or practice new words. Over time you will find that you have the ability to express your thoughts any way you want either in public speaking or in written communication. How do you express a complex idea if you can't find the right words to describe that idea? How do you expect others to understand what you are saying if you can't communicate it? How can others convey an idea to you if you can't understand what they are saying?

CHAPTER 4

NO MONEY, NO DOCTOR, NO LUNCH

I am nine years old now and in the fourth grade. My mother has been dead for almost two years, and things are pretty tough for me and my brothers. My father, now a single parent, is doing the best he can for us. He is working two low-paying jobs and has lost faith in many things in life, including doctors. If we got sick, we would just tough it out until we got well. Playing one dark night beside the railroad tracks in Lower Coast Algiers with a couple of friends, I suddenly felt a strange sensation in my right foot. For a moment I couldn't move; then suddenly came the pain. One of my friends had matches which he struck to see what was going on. I had become impaled on an eight-inch railroad spike; it was sticking out the top of my foot. Taking a quick look in the dim light of the match, one friend started to gag at the damage the spike had caused. Once we recovered from the shock, my friends pulled me off the spike and helped me to get home. By the time I reached home, my foot had swollen twice its size. No money. No doctor visit. No tetanus shot. However, my dad remembered the stories of home remedies that his father had used when he and his siblings were growing up. My grandfather was summoned, and when he arrived he made a poultice of crushed roaches and applied it to the wound. The poultice was changed several times, but before long there was no sign of swelling, and the wound started healing quickly. If you do an Internet search, you will find that this is now a known remedy for reducing swelling associated with wounds, and the crushed roaches also may have an "antiseptic" effect on bacteria.

My brothers and I were in elementary school all day without lunch money. Breakfast was pulling out some turnips from our grandfather's garden, shaking the dirt off the root, and eating them. This nourishment would have to last us until we got back home. Working in my grandfather's garden was a blessing. It afforded me the opportunity to learn the planting, growing, and reaping seasons of many vegetables. This knowledge, however, worked against me during the school's lunch period. The smell of the school lunch was wonderfully aromatic. To avoid thinking about being hungry, I would go to the school library and read the books there, all of them. I vowed to myself that I would read every book that the library had, no matter the subject. I signed the card in the back of the book to track my progress of which ones I had read and I just kept going. By the end of the school year, I had accomplished my goal—every book read.

The coping mechanism I used was just to get through the day. The knowledge and information that I was absorbing was preparing me for more horribly strenuous trials and tribulations to come.

No one, including my father, believed that I or my brothers would ever amount to anything. Dropping out of school and life was just around the corner for us. No one in the history of our family had ever graduated from high school. There was no perceived value or upside to staying in school. Opportunity for colored people did not exist back then except for janitors, the military, and school teachers.

Like many young people today, my older brother dropped out of school in the seventh grade. My younger brother dropped out in the fifth grade. To this day I still don't know why they quit. I always thought that they had more talent and intelligence than I did.

CHAPTER 5

NEVER GIVE UP

I'm in eighth grade now. The clothes I wear each day have been worn by someone else, so they don't fit well. They are very baggy and at times are torn in spots. The clothes are my older brother's hand-me-downs or ones we found at the city's dump site. The relatives, however, had a way of looking at things in a positive manner. Holes in your clothing was taken as a sign of purity of spirit. Finding something to wear that had been thrown away was considered good luck.

Every day as I walk past the school cafeteria, the food smells so wonderful. Once again there is a small problem; I have no money to buy lunch. As my stomach growls from hunger, there is nothing I can do. Wait a minute! I can go where I've gone so many times before, to my sanctuary, the school library and lose myself in the pages of a book, any book on any subject. This day, in the quiet of the library, I am able to reflect on my life and how far I've come and what lies in front of me. I would visualize a better existence for me although I didn't know what that future would hold.

I am also remembering back to when I was in the first grade trying to read and write at home. When I asked my parents for help, they couldn't. They could neither read nor write. I kept going over the strange words until they made sense to me. I learned how to glean the word's meaning from the context in the sentence. Then there was *division*; what a strange concept! It didn't make any sense to me because there was nothing in my reality to divide. Eventually I got the concept by using broken twigs and using them as my abacus.

Something interesting has been happening to me in elementary school. I have become proficient in reading and have shown an aptitude for mathematics. My teachers still parade me to other classes, so that I can read and solve various math problems they have written on the board. My growing knowledge and thoughts of all my possibilities were transforming me and telling me to never give up.

I don't know where my resolve to never give up or quit came from, but it has helped me through many, many difficult times. Time is the one real constant in our lives. Use it wisely every day. If we use our inner voice to say positive things, then positive things will happen. If we visualize what we really want our future to be, our subconscious and conscious mind will direct our efforts to achieve it.

A simple explanation or definition of visualization is the formation of a mental image or picture in the mind. When you visualize what you want, your subconscious mind begins working with the Universe to bring that to you. Today we know this process as *The Law of Attraction*. Visualizing is something you do every day without realizing. Don't think you do? Have you ever seen a car on the road that you would like to own? Next thing you know you are seeing that car everywhere. What about school or at work? You need to research a topic for a school paper or a work project and suddenly you begin seeing articles or receive emails on that very subject. Shortly after being diagnosed with diabetes, I started receiving great information through emails, pop-up advertisement on the Internet and even pamphlets by way of the US mail—all on how to control diabetes. Think about what you really want and never give up on that dream.

CHAPTER 6

THE ROAD I WALKED

I am thirteen years old now, and things have gotten even tougher for me. In fact it is one of the lowest points in my life. I now have a stepmom who believes in corporal punishment. She hasn't touched me yet, but she has beaten both my younger and older brothers. Stepmom has a temper and the simplest things set her anger off, and she would respond with violence. The last words I remember her saying the night before I left home forever was, "If I beat my own kids, you know I'll kill you." This was said as she threw my older brother against the refrigerator door punching and beating him repeatedly. I silently wished that she would attack and beat me because I knew I would retaliate back to her in kind. When my father got home from work that night I told him what had happened expecting some justice; there was none. He just sat at the kitchen table and hung his head. I could see no alternatives to my bad situation. I was too young to get a job and had no family or outside resources I could appeal to. My situation seemed to be totally helpless. It must have been about 1:00 a.m. when I made the decision to leave home.

The Dream

Our house was set on the edge of some very dense woods fronted by a clear stream fed by rainwater. That night, as I fell into a restless sleep, I had a vivid and detailed dream that felt very real. I saw an image of my deceased mother standing in a clear sparkling reflective stream. Her arms were reaching out to me as she spoke, "I know you are suffering and going through some pretty rough times. You can come into this stream and join me, which will end your suffering or you can stay in your world. If you choose to stay, I promise that your life will be wonderful."

As I walked into the kitchen the next morning I saw that my brothers, my dad, my stepmom, and her two kids were sitting at the breakfast table. There was one empty chair left for me. I silently looked at them in disgust, turned around, and left home with my belongings in a cardboard box. I never returned. I never looked back.

There was nowhere for me to go in this wooded area. I went to an abandoned camp with no windows, doors, or much of anything else. Then a miracle happened for me. My mom's sister had recently moved to Lower Coast Algiers from Port Sulphur, Louisiana for a job at Belle Chasse State School. She had no children of her own, and this lady was truly a saint. When she was told that I was living in the woods, she found me and told me to come live with her and her husband. It was a two-room shack, and I slept on the floor. Just when I thought things were looking up, the public-school bus that I rode was cancelled by the Orleans Parish School System because I wouldn't change schools. This meant that my daily walk to the nearest bus line was seven miles each way. I remember not ever thinking that this was too long a walk or too hard to do. I knew I had to do it to continue my education. My brothers who had dropped out of school continued to stay in that horrible home situation at home. My older brother died under mysterious circumstances, in a fire, in that same house. My younger brother became a laborer and didn't move out until he married. My undergraduate degree is a BA in psychology with a dual minor in mathematics and computer science. I also have an MBA from Tulane University.

Recent medical research has been able to prove the brain's healing powers from long walks. Walking and thinking for an hour or more has very beneficial effects on the body and mind. I didn't know it at the time, but the seven-mile walk to school every day was the absolute best activity for me at this point in my life. I would think and dream of where I wanted my life to go. The long walk never seemed to be a hardship for me; it was just the path I had to travel to get to school. If it was raining, I walked in it; if it was cold, I walked in that too. It didn't matter to me. My intellect was being further steeled against challenges, and my fortitude was being hardened by every stop that I took. By the time I was sixteen, I had a full-time job working from 4.00 p.m. to midnight. Eventually I was able to buy a used car which made getting around easier. I have a fundamental belief that we, as limitless human beings, will always have alternatives and solutions available to us in times of crisis.

CHAPTER 7

DIVINE GUIDANCE

It is so fascinating and illuminating to think back over my years of life and see clearly now how my path and journey was being guided by a higher power. A divine energy inside of me has always kept me focused on learning, growing, and helping others. Through my educational and work experiences there has always been someone who saw something in me. I have had many helping "guides" in my journey, and I have become a guide to many others.

My tenth-grade geometry teacher asked me to stand up in class one day for no apparent reason. I had been quietly sitting, like the other students, taking his pop quiz. After what seemed like unbearable minutes he stated to the class, "I don't know what David will do in the future with his life, but I do know that he will accomplish great things. He will be successful in whatever he chooses." I had no idea why this proclamation had been espoused by my teacher. I thought long and hard trying to figure out what brought about this comment.

We had just completed a class project where three-dimensional objects had to be constructed and turned in. I did not have money or means to buy material to build anything so I kept thinking. I did have paper and pencils. I began by drawing a three-dimensional picture of the earth using various geometric shapes to hold it up. Then I placed the earth and shapes in the palm of a human hand, holding everything up. It had to be my drawings that prompted his comment.

While at a fish fry one Friday night at an aunt's house she asked me, in front of all my cousins, "So you are still in high school? Are you going to stay in it and graduate?" My answer, "Yes I am." "And then what are you going to do?" she asked. To that I replied, "I'll probably go to college." On hearing this everybody on the porch started laughing so hard that some were in tears. This was1965—college and having a career were just unimaginable. My thoughts at the time were, "Why are they laughing and making fun of me?" As was the usual case in my life, I just shook off their negativity and said to myself, "They don't know who I am or what I will achieve!"

By the time of the fish fry, I had taken the preliminary Scholastic Aptitude Test. The following Monday morning my high-school counselor had come to visit me. It seemed that my test scores had raised the overall average for the entire school. I had won awards in art, physical education (P.E.), physics, and chemistry competitions. My counselor told me that if I stayed in school I might qualify for an academic scholarship to college.

What is a P.E. award doing among those for academic achievements you may ask? How did I get a P.E. award when, in my mind, I was a physical klutz? I felt this way all through high school. During those high-school years, there were no organized sports, in part, because there were no fields in which to play. How do you build a playing field in the swampy woody area I called home? So I had no idea how or why I received that award. In retrospect, I have three possible reasons.

The first could be because I merely showed up every day "dressed out" for gym with my shorts (one pair) and tee shirt on. I couldn't play basketball or football, and I had no interest in sports.

Secondly, maybe it was because of the day that I told my gym teacher that someone had stolen my tennis shoes out of my locker and pointed out the bully who was wearing them in the gym. He asked me, "What do you want me to do about that?"

I replied, "Make him give them back!"

His answer to that plea was, "Nope. If you want them, you go get them."

I asked him, "Do you mean that you are giving me permission to fight?"

He indicated with a nod of his head that he was giving me the go-ahead. So I walked out onto the gym floor to the bully and said, "Those are my shoes. Give them back."

Surprised by my boldness the bully simply replied, "Make me."

What happened next was a blur of fast punches and kicks. Within what seemed like one minute the guy gave up and handed my shoes back. As I looked around me, I was amazed that everyone in the gym had stopped their activities and started watching the fight. That bully became my friend. He told me later that he was really trying to beat me, but I was too fast for him. Me, fast? I had never considered that before.

Then there was the day I was late for P.E. If you were late for gym, the teacher made you take laps for punishment. Although I had the best explanation—meeting with the school counselor—I was told to run the required laps. Already on the track was the school's best runner. When I caught up to him, the sprint turned into a running match. For a short distance, we were neck and neck. Then with a spurt of speed, I reached the finish line first. I won! Once again the competition caught everyone's attention.

Maybe it was a combination of all three that I was able to prove my worthiness for the award. But more importantly I proved to myself that I could do something I had never thought I was capable of doing. We never know what we all are capable of doing in life until we try, until we make that attempt.

CHAPTER 8

ATTENTION TO SMALL DETAILS

The year is 1967, and my two best friends and I are walking on a dark lonely stretch of highway. The walk to get out of Lower Coast Algiers is about six miles in total, but we don't care. We are going to a party this Saturday night in the Cut Off (so named because Algiers, Louisiana was dissected by the Intracoastal Waterway).

A bright red two-door Chevrolet comes toward us flying past going in the opposite direction. The car was going faster than 100 mph, but everyone speeds on this straight stretch of dark highway. When the car stops about half a mile away from us, my friends recognize the vehicle as that of an uncle of mine. We assume that, as it turns around in the dark, he must be coming back to pick us up. As the car starts heading toward us, we can hear the engine roaring at maximum speed. My friends are excited and happy that we won't have to walk for another hour to get to town.

As the car's accelerator is rammed to the floor, I hear something. I hear the distinct grind of a manual transmission being shifted into a higher gear. My brain immediately said to myself, "Uncle's car has an automatic transmission."

It wasn't him! I had just enough time to yell to my friends to get out of the way. The car swerved violently trying to run over us; he missed.

How different my life, my friend's lives, my children, my forty-five-year career would have been if this stranger had succeeded in running us down? I would have been killed if I had reacted just a few seconds slower. I have always been able to pick up things that other don't see or notice. I learned early on to listen to my inner voice and act upon it.

There are always cues in our day-to-day environment telling us in nature's own way what we should be paying attention to. In today's world, there are a myriad of different distractions and noise. It has become harder than ever to pay attention to the realities around us. The Internet, four hundred TV channels, and smartphones are wonderful tools, but we should shut them off during periods where concentration and renewal of our psyche is needed.

Walking barefooted outside in nature is a first step in the renewing of both our minds and body. Modern scientific research has discovered that "earthing," as it is called, leads to many health benefits. Benefits include such things as improved health, some chronic pain relief, moderating heart rate variability, glucose regulation, and reduced stress. We completely block out this connection (electrons) between ourselves and Mother Earth by continually wearing shoes and only walking on concrete sidewalks. We need to "ground" ourselves a few times each week, so that our bodies can absorb these healthful electrons of the earth.

CHAPTER 9

HIGH-SCHOOL GRADUATION

I am sitting in the high-school auditorium waiting for our ceremony to begin. I look around at my classmates and know that I will never see many of them again. For some of them, this is the end of their educational journey. I see relief on their faces, glad that they will no longer have to attend school. On others, I see excitement for the future. They are not moving on to college but will be entering the workforce. Then there are those like myself who will be moving on to college. My high school covered from the seventh grade through the twelfth grade. Of that entire class of 135 students, only thirty-six of us were selected to participate in an experimental group for a special curriculum that would prepare us for college. Again, just a stroke of good fortune. I loved the academic challenges of being taught differently and being labeled special. For me it made my high-school experience much more rewarding. Of the thirty-six class members, thirty-five went on to attend college. What emotions are going through our minds? They are mixed. Some relief, some excitement, and some fear of not knowing what our futures hold.

The principal walks out onto the stage to give us a farewell speech. The speech is filled with words of encouragement, praise for the teachers, and sentimental feelings of leaving school. When his speech is concluded, the diplomas are readied for the students' names to be called. As our names are called by the principal, he announces each student's accomplishments. My name is now being called. As I begin my walk down the aisle, on my way to the stage to receive my diploma, I hear the principal announce that I have earned a full academic scholarship to Southern University in architectural engineering. In fact, it is the only competitive academic scholarship achieved in the class. It seems that my IQ and SAT scores are some of the best in the nation.

As I continue to stroll slowly to the stage, following the cadence of the graduation music, I hear a classmate's mom say, "I thought he was dumb." I smile to myself with a sense of satisfaction as I reflect on this lady's words and remember the harsh words spoken at my mother's funeral, "These kids are doomed because their mother is dead." There are two types of people I have found: those who raise you up and those who try to tear you down. Do not hang around doom-and-gloom personality types. Negativity really wears your psyche down like a two-ton weight around your neck pulling you underwater.

One of the cultural artifacts that was evident all around me was people saying negative things about everyone else. I heard the negative comments and saw the results of all the self-hate that existed among our people. I still see it today but don't buy into it, never did, and never will.

Psychologically, every human being needs to have a sense of self-worth. Unfortunately, we often satisfy that need by minimizing others around us. It could be hurtful words thrown at us from family members, relatives, friends, or even strangers. There was bad programming in my culture that just sucked the life and hope out of everyone. Flash-forward to today. The horrible times of us not respecting ourselves or others is coming back full force. Guns are everywhere, and we are indiscriminately shooting one another. Our music contains vulgar and demeaning lyrics, and females are called by disrespectful names. With all the everyday tragedies we currently see in our country, we must care for each other more than ever. We need to know and understand that all the negative crap being spewed by our politicians is just that—crap! So many things are said and facts twisted to suit an agenda, and that agenda is not always in our own best interest.

Another source of academic aid that should have been available to me was a UNCF scholarship. I was denied, as informed by my school counselor, because the fund stated that with my IQ score I wouldn't need any assistance. I considered this erroneous and unfair statement for a moment but chose to shake it off and move on.

CHAPTER 10

FULL-TIME STUDENT AND EMPLOYEE

Earlier I mentioned what a blessing it was to have my aunt move from Port Sulphur, Louisiana, to the Lower Coast Algiers to take a job. The position at the state school was as a cook. I remember how she was able to cook the most wondrously aromatic dishes for our family. My aunt, like most of the elders in our family, could not read or write. At times she would be asked to prepare dishes at the school she was unfamiliar with. All that was necessary was showing her a picture to work from and she would be able to create a nutritious meal for the children. Her working at the state school turned out to be a piece of good fortune for me very soon.

Lower Coast Algiers was nothing but a swampy area with not much land on which you could build a business. In fact, there were no businesses. The state school for children, however, was able to open in this area. Upon hearing that the school was hiring, I decided to apply for a position that became available. If hired, I would work the 11:00 p.m. to 7:00 a.m. shift as a residential monitor. In addition to the application, there would also be an aptitude test. I completed both the application and test answering everything correctly and honestly, well almost. I knew that to work full-time you had to be eighteen years old, so I put down that I was twenty-four. I was interviewed and got the job. Now I had the means to feed and take care of myself. This also meant that I would be taking my normal school classes while working full-time. After leaving school I would go home and do homework for a bit, then sleep for a few hours until it was time to go to work. I was also able to read and study while at work when time permitted.

The work was very rewarding. I had the opportunity to see kids who had special needs and kids who were placed in the facility because their families didn't want to be bothered with them. Their emotions were pure. If it was anger, you knew it. If it was love, you saw it. My duties consisted of monitoring the children, from a central location, at night while they slept in their dormitories and handling anything that might arise during the shift. Given my background, I could relate to their circumstances which made it very easy to bond with the kids and understand what they were feeling and why they behaved as they did.

Nights at work were usually very quiet unless something had happened during the day to upset a child. One evening such an event took place on a dark Sunday night. If you really want to see what darkness looks like go into a forest at night. It is so dark you are unable to see your hand held directly in front of your face. There were only two of us working that Sunday night. It must have been about 2:00 a.m. when we heard loud noises emanating from the dormitory bathroom. The other orderly rushed with me into the bathroom area and saw that a face bowl had been ripped off the wall with water gushing all over the place from the busted pipe. We frantically looked for the shut off valve to stop the torrent, found it, and turned off the water. In that quiet moment we looked at each other and realized that we had left the door to the control room open. Bobby had escaped the dormitory and ran off into the woods! Bobby was someone who would get upset and act out after a visit from his parents. We are usually notified when this occurrence happens but not this night. Bobby was once again upset that his parents had left him. We locked the doors and ran outside to try and find Bobby.

My co-worker was a big strong man who had been a star defensive end in high school. I told him to go in one direction and I would take the other. It was pitch black. I listened intently to the sounds of the woods and heard footsteps behind me. I thought it was Bobby stalking me! It was my co-worker. I told him, "You were supposed to go in the opposite direction."

He replied, "No way am I going into these woods without you."

Just then I heard noises in front of me. We ran toward the noises and there he was: Bobby, totally naked standing on a log. (Bobby also had a habit of ripping off his clothes.) Now what do we do to get him back to the dormitory?

My mind raced and I yelled to Bobby, "If you can catch me, you can beat me up!"

He began to chase after me. My co-worker just looked at me in awe as we ran past Bobby heading back to the dormitory. As I entered the building I stayed just far enough ahead of Bobby to make him think that he could catch me.

I entered the dormitory and high-jumped over a four-foot railing. I was able to make a circle to get back to the control area and lock the door. From the microphone in the control room I told Bobby to get in his bed and he did.

The next day my supervisor said, "I hear you guys had some excitement last night!"

I replied with a simple, "Yes, we did."

She smiled and said, "Good job."

She then told me the story of the day when she had been struck in the neck area by Bobby and how the blow had broken a bone in her neck. I said that must have been terrible. She replied not really. The treating physician had the area of the blow x-rayed, and a tumor was discovered. The tumor was caught early enough that it was treated and then removed. If not for that blow and early detection, the tumor would have gone unnoticed and would have probably killed her. There are often positive outcomes from situations that are invisible to us at the moment of their occurrence.

I heard some years later that, while on one of his excursions outside of the school, Bobby was hit by a car and died. Sad, he was such a loving child.

CHAPTER 11

DECISIONS

My senior year of high school turned out to be a very hectic time for me. My counselor was keeping me informed of the several universities that were interested in offering me academic scholarships which included military academies. This is usually a heady time for seniors, their parents, and extended family. Sitting down and discussing the college opportunities was a luxury I did not have. By this time I had already moved from home, so I had no support. Although I had many choices of schools, there was only one option. I knew that I couldn't take offers as far away as Idaho (University of Idaho) or for that matter any college, including military academies, that were located out of state. Going out of state would mean finding funding for transportation to school and back home. I would also have to pay any cost that the scholarship did not cover. I could, of course, find a job to provide for those necessities, but I knew it would never be enough for all expenditures. So I made the only decision available; I chose Southern University in Baton Rouge, Louisiana. One of the scholarships Southern offered me was in engineering, any type. Since my first love had always been art, I chose architectural engineering.

The transition from high-school student and full-time worker to that of a full-time college student was shocking to me. It seemed that now everything in my small world had changed. The cultural and social scene in college was something I had never imagined. Living in a college dorm with four roommates was not what I had expected. They all came from good families with a great support system. Since I had neither family nor support I was considered a lone wolf. The academic work was surprisingly easy to me, and I made it to the Dean's list in my first semester. During that first semester, we were assigned various architectural projects to create. Not having the funds to buy construction materials was a challenge. I made sculptures and drawings out of scrap or anything that I could find lying around. One of my instructors was German and named "Wolfe." He was a no-nonsense, tough professor. His grading system was the toughest I had ever encountered. There were about thirty students in the class and only one "A" could be awarded to a specific project and each student got to arrange them from number one to number thirty. We all had a vote. I was amazed and pleased when my designs and drawings made it to the number-one position! I could not fathom where or how these creations came out of me but they did. The second semester I became restless, and my funds had just about run out. The last meal was served on Sunday at noon in the school cafeteria, and I had to go without until 8.00 a.m. Monday morning for my next meal, breakfast. At this point I decided to quit college and go back home to New Orleans. It was a decision that could very well impact my whole future for it was the height of the Vietnam War.

What school to attend and career path to take were not the only decisions I had to make in my senior year. I also had to inform my employer, the state school, that I was leaving to attend college. When I gave my two-week notice there was some shock on the part of my co-workers. By their account I would have been a twenty-six-year old just graduating from high school. They didn't even believe me when I confessed that I was only seventeen. I had to show them my driver's license as proof of my age. I apologized for the deception but I had needed the job; I had to work. Not everyone was surprised. My supervisor didn't bat an eye when I told her of my departure for college. Her reaction was not quite what I had expected. In fact, she provided some sound advice. She told me to take my time and consider all options before choosing a major. Then I was surprised by her suggestion that I consider going into medicine. Although she favored a career in medicine, she told me of her struggles as a woman in her early days as a med student and intern. I quickly dismissed this idea because of my situation. I was impatient about getting on with my life and getting through school as quickly as possible. I thanked her for her support, and I left her office with a tear in my eye. I had learned a lot about human nature, and although I loved this job something kept pushing me forward in my life. I often wonder if this was a missed opportunity. Today I follow many new breakthroughs in medicine and science. Could I have found a way to make medicine a career?

CHAPTER 12

A FORTY-FIVE-YEAR CAREER BEGINS

Since leaving college I have had my military student deferral revoked. I have taken my military physical and IQ tests at the Custom House in New Orleans and I am rated 1A—ready for combat. An Army recruiter meets with me and says that because of my high test scores I can have training in any of the three hundred job assignments they have.

I ask, "Got anything related to Physics?" He laughs and suggests dentistry.

I laugh and say, "I'll think about it."

He states seriously, "You have twenty-one days to decide or I promise you front-line combat duty in Vietnam." (This is the same promise of front-line duty my ROTC commander made when I told him I was leaving college.)

I think to myself, "Okay, I came up hunting, fishing, and surviving off the land. I can survive this too." I envisioned keeping my firearms with me at the ready at all times, even while sleeping.

One of my first cousins was getting married in a Catholic church in Plaquemine parish and asked me to stand in his wedding. The wedding date was very close and I initially refused, but he kept insisting. I finally agreed, and he told me where to rent the tuxedo. I didn't have a penny, so I figured I'd find a job for two weeks and earn enough to pay for the tux rental. I checked the newspaper's "Help wanted" section and found a help-wanted ad for a local telephone company. The ad said they were seeking applicants with mathematics background. The advertised position was for an outside cable repairman's helper. This appealed to me and seemed perfect. After all it would just be for two weeks.

I arrived at the employment office at 8:00 a.m. and completed an application. I was told to take a seat and to wait for my name to be called. At 8:45 a.m. my name is called, and I'm given an aptitude test. No problem. I answer all the questions and wait. I am given another test, again no problem, I finish and I wait. I am given another test and then another. Although it is getting late in the day I am, however, enjoying the diversity of subjects I am being given. I have taken at least six tests and have only been given enough time to go to the restroom. Years later I will find out what this is all about. And yes, I got the job. I am in that employment office until 5:30 p.m. At that time I am told to come back the next day to speak to the hiring recruiter.

The next day when I sat down with the recruiter, she said that after reviewing my test scores she had decided that rather than placing me in the outside job she was assigning me to a position in the "Central Office." I had no idea, or cared, what this term meant; after all, it was my intention to only be there for a couple of weeks.

I am reporting to my new job, but I have no idea what a Central Office Frameman, a semiskilled technician does.

I thought I would be "framing" something. The work I am learning is fascinating and easy to do. The original two weeks have passed, my cousin's wedding went well, and I am still working and receiving a regular paycheck. The Army recruiter's words still play in my mind every day, "Choose a career or you get front-line combat." After about three weeks I start calling the Army Recruiting office. I keep getting sixty IPMs, that's telephone talk for a busy signal. I once try to get through for a solid hour with no luck. Out of frustration I decide to just wait for the military draft. Call Waiting, Automatic Call Back, and Call Forwarding Busy didn't exist yet; all you got was a busy signal. The company I worked for was one of those rare companies that if an employee was designated as 1A they would hold a job for you upon your return from military service. The magic of being in the perfect environment for development, learning, and challenge has begun for me. The number of absolutely fantastic people I started meeting over forty-five years ago is amazing. They are still my friends and guiding lights today. The military draft never called me. They had started a "draft lottery" system, and my number was 286. They called draftees up to 280 that year. The whole time line of my life would have been different if not for a telephone-busy signal.

CHAPTER 13

BALANCING COLLEGE AND WORK

I found myself at nineteen years old restarting college at Southern University in New Orleans while working full-time from 4:00 p.m. to midnight. I had earned another full academic scholarship and changed my major from architectural engineering to my second academic love, physics.

The first lesson I had to learn was how to balance work, school, desires, and outcomes. It wasn't easy working a full-time job, carrying at one point a full load of twenty-two credit hours and having a few friends I wanted to spend time with. I realized that in order for me to obtain my college degree there were sacrifices I would have to make. When I got off at midnight I would stop at one of the small Seven-Eleven convenience stores, buy a half pint of milk and a Mrs. Drake's sandwich from the cold vending case. Since the sandwiches were cold from a day's refrigeration and with no means of heating them I learned to eat my food cold. That was dinner every night. When I arrived home around 12:30 a.m. I'd allocate two hours for study and four hours for sleep. This routine did not seem extremely difficult to me; it was after all, what I had to do in order to achieve my goal of college graduation. There were many false starts. My work hours changed sometimes after I had gone far into a semester. This meant I had to withdraw and start over next semester. It also meant sometimes going to school in the evenings, daytime, or on weekends. It was the constancy of purpose that kept me focused especially when my friends wanted to go out on the weekends to have a good time. Very seldom did I participate in social events; there wasn't much time left in the day to participate in such activities.

Considering the amount of time I would need to accomplish my studies and prepare for exams I chose to make those sacrifices. Sacrifice is the wrong word, an incorrect word. I had to make those decisions that would further me toward my goal of graduating. Constancy of purpose, I knew I had to complete these courses, pass these courses, and keep pushing forward. My reward to myself for an "A" on an exam would be lunch at my favorite Chinese restaurant. A bowl of hot and sour soup and Moo Goo Gai Pan was a treat, but only if I did well on my exams. There were times when I couldn't eat lunch because I needed the time to study. There were times when I couldn't get four hours of sleep because I needed to pull an all-nighter. I felt blessed to find in life the ability of prioritization, of putting first things first.

Prioritization really lets you accomplish whatever goal or objective you are trying to achieve. I never thought this was difficult or hard (a theme throughout my life). I never felt I was deprived of anything because I couldn't have a hot meal after coming home from work. I just kept pushing forward until I graduated.

As human beings we have the mental capacity to focus and strive for whatever is important to us. We can control our thoughts and choose to have a positive attitude toward challenges and problems. Amid all the noise we are surrounded by, there will be solutions there too.

CHAPTER 14

THE POWER OF YOUR THOUGHTS

The true power that has made a difference in my life is that my thoughts have always been positive. Many people I have met for the first time say, "I feel like I know you." When I meet people, total strangers, it doesn't take me very long to connect with them and we find some commonalities. Even though I wasn't really aware of it myself people would always come back to me and say, "You're so positive about everything." The point I am trying to make here is that we have to be careful what we think. A lot of brain research is now showing that the subconscious mind is always listening to what the conscious mind is saying. If you really want to change or accomplish something you should say it, visualize it, feel it, believe it, and repeat it. Don't let the negative thoughts creep into your mind that you can't do something. Don't let the negative messages coming through the media and social networks define your morale and sense of who you are. I remember reading a study a few years ago that said every day we have over forty thousand different thoughts and on average about 80 percent are negative, totally negative. So you can see how this would tend to make whatever you want to change, whatever endeavor you want to tackle even more difficult. By knowing that this negativity is a natural reflex you can change it by turning it to a positive. When the negative thought creeps into your conscious mind change the thought. The more you practice this the easier it becomes to maintain a positive attitude.

If you look at successful people around you or successful businesses, you will see that they were all challenged with and overcame "can't do it, can't be done." Here are a few examples. Through their vision and belief in their dream, the Wright Brothers overcame "man will never fly" and ushered in the age of air travel. Our dream of space travel was once only science fiction. Now NASA is planning a trip to Mars. Since our scientists have verbalized this plan, the details and challenges are being solved. More powerful rocket engines, needed for long distance travel, are being developed and tested. Tests are being performed on astronauts to determine what the effects would be on the human body's functions during very long stints in space. If not for our vision, determination, and perseverance we would never have witnessed our first steps on the moon. The list goes on and on. As soon as these blinders are taken off then you too will be released to accomplish great things.

Again my blessing is that I don't listen to the voices of self-doubt that say, "It can't be done." I can remember in a calculus class being confronted with a really tough problem. I'd just grind on it until I got the answer. Then I would work the problem a few times until it became automatic and then the insight would come which allowed me to work more difficult problems. During a physics lab experiment in college, I was conducting a spectroscopic analysis of background radiation in the environment. I knew the reference number that I should be receiving, but I kept getting a higher radiation reading. My professor kept rejecting my work and said to run the experiment again. He sent me back to the physics lab seven times. I began to get frustrated, and it was getting late into the evening. I double- and triple-checked the equipment calibration and it was perfect. I took a few deep breaths and looked at my chronograph watch on my wrist. It had gotten so dark in the dimly lit lab that I had to push the background light button on my watch to see the time. Then it hit me, the watch used radium for illumination! Radium 223 is highly radioactive and therefore it is not used in watches any longer. I took the watch off, put it into a lead shield and measured again. This time the reading was perfect. I never forgot this lesson. Answers to many of life's challenges are right in front of us if we just keep searching.

Space, mathematics, and physics are but a few examples where imagination, the power of positive thoughts, and a "can do" attitude won the day. This viewpoint works in any field we choose, and it works in our day-to-day life. The more you practice this "yes I can" attitude, the more natural or second nature it becomes.

CHAPTER 15

BELIEVE THERE ARE ALWAYS ALTERNATIVES

I have found that as we try to change circumstances around us there are always roadblocks to our progress. These roadblocks always seem to pop up at the most inopportune times. It's as if nature wants to keep us at the equilibrium point that we are at. You must expect these challenges and think about what options you have. I've believed all my life that there are always alternatives to whatever situation is presented to us. When you are trying to change something or push to a higher level, there are, at times, obstacles that just seem to get in the way. I know that when challenges present themselves it usually means that you are right at the precipice of pushing through, of getting out of the cave, the dungeon and walking into the sunlight.

Having lived in Louisiana my entire life, I find the same types of challenges. We have been challenged with hurricanes over the years and it seems more repeatedly of late. But after every hurricane does its damage, there is always a rebirth, a renewal, a spring that comes to everything. It is truly during times of adversity that we define who we are to ourselves, and we determine who we are to others. When everything is going smoothly and quietly we are not being challenged as human beings. We need these challenges and adversity to learn and grow. Only then do we gain insight and strength of character.

There is no limit to our strength of character and ability to grow. We just have to truly believe in ourselves and keep on striving. Nature intends for human beings to keep advancing and striving. There is such a waste of human potential when an individual doesn't get an education or gets incarcerated repeatedly. Our society is losing too many people this way. With the Internet and the access we now have to the information and wisdom of the world, there should be no excuse for not learning every day, getting smarter every day.

We may not like some of the alternatives that are presented to us in a given situation, but I have found that sometimes it may take years before we can appreciate that the road taken was the best choice. For example, when I withdrew from the university during my second semester I had no idea that I would earn another full academic scholarship and find a job that both challenged me and taught me so many leading-edge technical things. It also taught me how to lead and motivate the people in my organizations.

CHAPTER 16

HOW I BECAME HUMAN RESOURCE DIRECTOR AND WHAT I LEARNED FROM THE THREE-YEAR EXPERIENCE

After obtaining my MBA degree I was promoted to director of network operations and engineering. It was the technical department that operates seven days a week and twenty-four hours a day. Everyone in this department knew how critical their role was in providing telephone service to our customers. This promotion was in year twenty-three of my telecommunication career; a career that began when I was only eighteen years old. I had started as a semi-skilled technician, later to be promoted to supervisor, then manager and finally to director. Working full-time in a very challenging job and going to graduate school was tough, but I was used to the grind from my past endeavors. After graduation from the MBA program I thought to myself, "Now what lies ahead?" A couple of weeks later my boss called me to say that someone from Corporate Human Resources in Atlanta was flying in to interview me. Astonished and somewhat confused I asked my boss, "For what reason?" He replied that they wanted to interview me to be the head of Human Resources (HR) for the state of Louisiana. He said that since I had been this intensely technical leader for my whole career Corporate wanted to give me a two- to three-year rotational assignment in order to develop my softer people skills. The Human Resources Director position, at this point in time, was perceived to be very powerful and unique within the company. I had always been interested in doing more for our employee body, and I felt that this was the perfect opportunity to do so. I asked my boss, "What do I need to do next?" He replied that I should call, John, the Corporate HR General Manager. So I called.

John answered my call, and we had a good conversation on general topics. We then proceeded to discuss his upcoming visit. I was to pick him up at the airport Friday morning, and he would then conduct the interview over lunch. After lunch and interview I would drive him back to the airport. At the end of the phone call, John posed an interesting question. He wanted to know how we would recognize each other. "John, I'd like to show you something. I always like to see if I can connect to people, feel them out, and guess what they do for a living. Do not describe yourself to me, and I will pick you out of the crowd after you come out of the gate." John was intrigued by this game and agreed to participate but provided his cell phone number in case I couldn't pick him out.

I arrived at the Delta Airline's gate fifteen minutes early and waited for the plane to land. As people began to come through the gate, I saw a young man who had a very dignified air about him. I walked up to him and said, "Hello John, how was your flight? I am David Butler." Needless to say he was quite amused and amazed. That's the way our entire meeting went. We had many great conversations about many topics. I drove him back to the airport, and he told me that he would let me know his decision the following week. Monday morning I received a call from John informing me that I was the new HR director for Louisiana.

My new corner office was at Canal Place in New Orleans on the eighteenth floor. Out one window I had a spectacular view of the city. Looking out from another window I could see the Mississippi River as it curved before straightening on its way south toward the Gulf of Mexico. What beautiful views! For three days the incumbent HR director, a very sweet and reserved gentleman, gave me an overview of the job along with a few pointers. For those three days, we had peace and quiet. The telephone was silent, and there were no tidal waves of incoming e-mails, something I'm now sure he had arranged. The pace of the day seemed very sedentary and I thought to myself, "Wow, after being on call twenty-four hours a day seven days a week for years this is really different." I had another thought that this was going to be an easy assignment. Was I ever more wrong? The next week the incumbent HR director retired, and I officially became the HR director for Louisiana. Within days my telephone started ringing constantly with various departmental issues and problems. There was a backlog of labor grievances between the union and the company that numbered in the thousands and a myriad of issues were going on. Some of those issues were literally life and death situations. I handled everything in Human Resources which included but not limited to legal arbitrations, mediations, affirmative action, discrimination charges, legal cases, employee benefits, accident investigations, and environmental hazards. If you can name it, I had it. I learned on the job very quickly, and I enjoyed it.

The biggest thing I learned from the assignment is that when in HR many times you are a little late influencing the prevention of a situation that caused the problem. I often felt like someone arriving at the scene of a head-on collision rather than preventing the accident. Just like drivers need to learn to recognize blind spots to avoid accidents, so must management realize what turmoil can be created by avoiding personnel issues. Better to handle these problems before they become head-on collisions. Another important lesson was keeping a balance between the company's interest and the well-being of the employees.

After spending my three years in HR I went to my boss, actually my boss's boss in Atlanta, to discuss my return to network operations. He proceeded to tell me that since there was no written agreement that the HR assignment was rotational, they were going to keep me in HR permanently. I would receive a promotion and a transfer to Atlanta headquarters to handle arbitration cases for all nine states against the labor union. I saw this as being one-dimensional and said, "No thanks." I wanted to go back to network operations but was told, "You don't have a contract. You're are not going back." I did, however, have a verbal agreement. I made a call to my General Manager in network operations who escalated to the state President. I was soon sent back to network operations in New Orleans. I never discovered why that strange incident happened. Being the VP of HR that person had to know we did rotational assignments all the time and that verbal agreements were binding.

Whenever you are about to join a new company or start a new job assignment within a company, there are a few approaches that always seem to work.

1. Go in with no preconceived notions. In other words, keep your eyes and ears open. This is your first opportunity to listen and learn. What is the culture like?
2. Meet with your boss and ask what she or he expects from you quickly. What are the things that need improvement immediately? What are the pain points as things currently exist?
3. Meet with your peers or departmental interfaces and ask their perspective on operations.
4. If in a managerial position, meet with your employees and ask them what needs to be worked on. Draw up an action plan from this input and develop it into a project plan.
5. Give feedback as to what your course of action will be. Ascertain what success looks like and be sure to communicate this up and down the chain of command.
6. After a month or two, ask for feedback from your boss as to how you are performing.
7. Make course corrections and start the process all over again. This feedback never ends, and it keeps communications open and flowing.

Take every opportunity that is offered to you. It's your chance to learn and grow. You often never know where these opportunities will lead in your future. What may look to you like a step backward can be many steps forward.

CHAPTER 17

HOW THE THREAD OF LIFE RUNS THROUGH EVERYTHING

As a twenty-three year old supervisor of a group of employees, some who were more than double my age and experience, I learned early on about the importance of "leading by example" to influence others. A blood drive was being conducted at work, and we were all being encouraged to schedule a time to donate. I had never donated blood in my life, and I never intended to start now. I was afraid of the needle. I knew what the human blood types were (A, B, AB, and O) and the Rh (Rhesus) factor from biology class but had never had mine typed. I often wondered what my blood type was, however, I always felt that my blood would be one of the rarer types.

When the day of the blood drive arrived, I still had not signed up to donate. One of my direct reports teased me unmercifully about being afraid to donate. Joe was my mentor before the term existed as we know it today. He would lock onto something that I needed to do in order to improve myself and would never let it go until I made the change.

There were some things that he reminded me of monthly, weekly, or daily. Donating blood was one of those things. To get him off my case, I relented. After being drained of the pint of blood, I was given a small cup of orange juice and told to get up from the cot. I told the nurse that I heard a loud ringing in my ears and she said harshly, "No you don't!" As I began to pass out on my feet, my last thought was to fall toward her with the cup of juice thrown in her direction. After ten minutes of lying on the cot, I was able to get up. Later I was told that my orange juice was a direct hit on the nurse's nice white tunic.

The next day after this traumatic event I noticed how energetic and good I felt both mentally and physically. Years later in discussing with my doctor how great I felt after donating blood, he explained to me that we males have too much iron in our blood at times, and we have no natural means to get rid of it. Donating a pint of blood accomplishes this. The body regenerates new cells and iron levels are reset. A couple of weeks after the blood drive, my blood type card arrived in the mail. My blood type is AB positive. The positive portion of the blood type is the Rh factor. The Rh factor is either positive or negative depending on whether there is an inherited protein on the surface of the red blood cells. Only 3 percent of the population in the world has this type of blood. My feelings of having a rare type of blood had been correct.

Over the years of my life I have been frequently called upon to donate blood to help people with life-threatening needs for AB positive blood. A wounded police officer who needed many transfusions, a nine-year-old child fighting for his life battling leukemia, and a co-worker's mother needing platelets in her struggle against cancer, all required the gift of life. I donated every time and as often as I could. I still do to this today.

Once as I sat at Mary Bird Perkins Hospital waiting to donate, I had the opportunity to speak with many sick people. As we talked, the gratitude and hope they expressed was very inspiring to me. They were so grateful for my act of donation, and I had the benefit of feeling great after the procedure was completed. Every small act that we do can have huge ramifications in the future. Actions and ideas have energy surrounding them that seem to carry on forever. Doing good deeds carry the benefit forward with powerful momentum forever in time.

What about that initial blood donation? Several of my co-workers came with Joe and I not only to see me donate for the first time but also to see me face my fear of the big needle. And yes, they also signed up to donate.

We now know through brain research and magnetic resonance imaging that humans as well as many other species exhibit mirror neurons. We can influence others through our actions being observed and this phenomenon is how we can read other people's minds and feel empathy for them.

CHAPTER 18

ALL-DAY TESTING AFFAIR

In chapter 12, I mentioned how I was tested all day for my first job in the communications industry. I reported to the employment office as instructed at 8:00 a.m. That day there were about fifty to sixty other applicants sitting and waiting to be interviewed or tested. As I sat and waited for my name to be called, I glanced around the room but to my surprise couldn't find anyone who looked like me. At eight fifteen, my name was called with a few others and we were led to a small room where we were given an aptitude test. We were allowed thirty minutes to complete the written test. I was able to complete the test in twenty minutes and allowed to return to the main waiting room. A few minutes after taking a seat, I was called to the front desk, led away, and given another test instrument. Thirty minutes later, I was back in the main room sitting. This process was repeated throughout the day. Each time upon returning to the main room, I noticed that the number of applicants was growing smaller. Throughout the long day there were no breaks or a lunch period, only a few minutes between tests to use the restroom.

It was 5:30 p.m. and there were only two or three people left from the original fifty to sixty who started in the morning. I was called up to the front desk and told to come back the next day to learn of my assignment. I thought all this wasted time for a job I intended to keep just for two weeks and then off to the military. The next day I was given the Central Office Technician (inside) position, not the Lineman's helper (outside plant) job I had applied for. The Human Resource job interviewer said that because of my testing results she felt that I would do better in a more complex job.

One more step remained before being hired, a physical exam. After a full day of mental testing now I just had to pass my physical. Back then an applicant had to be within their ideal weight range, pass an eye test, balance test, etc. During the eye exam, the optometrist excitedly called the other doctors in the office to re-examine and verify his findings. I wondered what was causing what appeared to me as concern on all their faces. The optometrist who originally examined me smiled and said that they rarely get patients who have perfect vision and eye muscles. I was relieved.

About ten years later while I was job shadowing the HR manager I learned the procedures for job testing and placement. One test and you are done. "That is not what I experienced," I said. I thought for a few minutes before asking politely, "Why did I have to take at least six or more tests?" His answer stunned me.

He said, "In order to reject or control the amount of minority applicants they would test until you failed. Since you continued to pass test after test they had no alternative but to hire."

A few years later the company would come under a "consent decree" from the federal government where there were certain diversity goals that had to be met. I remember the decree where the company's statement was that they were only doing what other companies in the United States were doing. This company later became a leader in treating people fairly and advancing careers based upon training, performance, and potential.

The training I received over the years was diverse and quite extensive. The training material alone would have reached a height of fifty feet. Courses I completed were in subjects such as electronics, switching technologies, achieving peak performance, Internet Protocol theory, analyzing data, and public speaking. I absorbed all that I could each year. I also made sure that my work-groups also got access to training that stretched and developed their abilities. New job titles and responsibilities kept flying my way. People enjoyed working with me and for me. I enjoyed putting them first and seeing their growth.

As human beings we should take every opportunity to learn and grow in every possible way that we can. Always stay open to new opportunities and options. There is no finite limit as to how much we can learn. I still learn new things every day, and this helps me to have a broad perspective on matters of importance.

CHAPTER 19

CHALLENGES IN LIFE DEVELOP WHO WE ARE INTERNALLY AND EXTERNALLY

You cannot fully comprehend how life's experiences in one moment in time will affect you and those around you at another moment in time. The thread of time and events are continuous for each of us and those close to us. Oftentimes it takes months or even years for us to see how some decision or an indecision, in a single moment, can have an impact that will carry forward in years to come. The thread of change and time are continuous for each of us. Keeping ourselves open and positive to inevitable change is the best way to get more joy and fulfillment out of life.

By the time I had risen in my company to the level of a senior executive, which included fantastic perks and pay, I began to notice that our company culture was changing rapidly and not for the better. With the passing of the Telecommunications Act of 1996, which reduced regulation and promoted competition within the industry, the company's downsizing initiatives were taking a tremendous toll on everyone involved. People became fearful in keeping their jobs. We began to terminate good employees by the thousands. Every day I could see the debilitating effects of hardship and stress of facing the unknown. During this time of turmoil, outside consultants had convinced company leaders that the coming deregulation and competition would take away a large percentage of our market share and customers. Long before the arrival of viable competitors, a second round of workforce reductions began. I saw this as an opportunity to redeploy our human resources but many companies, mine included, believed that downsizing was the only way to react. This began the company's death spiral. Once again, my position with the company was very secure, but it was like being in the eye of a hurricane. Very calm in the "eye" that I was in but all hell breaking loose around me. I saw the damage that was done to employee morale and productivity. I saw employee behavior become obtuse as they became more fearful of their future; they were terrified of the unknown. The company did not do a good job in managing the psychological damage that they were causing.

I was one of the leaders tasked to implement some of our reengineering projects and quality improvement initiatives. These efforts always had a bottom line of more reductions in people. As a leader my company had sent me to one of William Deming's Quality seminars. Deming was regarded as the creator of the "Quality" improvement process used throughout the world. His methods had helped rebuild Japan after World War II. Japan's motor vehicles such as by Toyota and others were literally junk and filled with many major defects. Through his leadership and improvement processes Japanese motor vehicles quickly surpassed

American-made motor vehicles in quality and performance. One of his first tenets in implementing a quality/process improvement program was to make the workforce feel safe about their jobs. We did not do this. It made the whole process seem dishonest. Because I was the leader on several of these projects, I became the company spokesperson for the company reductions in my state. I felt like the grim reaper standing in front of hundreds of people knowing that their lives were about to be altered.

One day, in the midst of this process, I woke up with a 104-degree fever. I was so proud of my twenty-plus years of never missing a day of work, so I got up and went in to work that day. Sitting at one end of a conference room table, so as not to breathe on anyone, our local management team met to discuss company direction and strategy. At the close of the meeting my boss, sitting at the other end of the table, pointed to me and said, "I don't care what you have to do or take, but it is critical that you drive to the meeting tomorrow morning!" That meeting was 152 miles away and in reality was not all that important. It was a perfunctory meeting that was held every month. It was at that moment in time that I decided to walk away from that company.

I had no idea what I would do next with my life. There were projects around the house that I never had time to start or complete. I spent the next six months painting my wood-and-brick frame house. I also got involved in projects around the neighborhood because the neighbors knew that I wasn't working any longer. One day a neighbor's wife came to the door and asked me to help her husband, who had Parkinson's disease, put a big-ass, self-propelled lawn mower into the trunk of their Toyota Corolla. The husband's hands were shaking so badly that he couldn't lift anything, so I asked him to step back and let me lift the lawn mower alone. While lifting the lawn mower, I felt a sharp pain in my back. I already had two back discs that had given me pain for over twenty years. Now I had completely ruptured one of them. The pain was the worst thing I had ever felt. Because of my upbringing, I had built up a high tolerance for pain, but this was something different. The pain was so severe that I could hear it as it washed over me like a dark cloud. It sounded like the roar of an ocean wave cascading over me. For a week I tried to get over it but nothing changed. I finally went to see a neurosurgeon and had a MRI. It was a totally ruptured L5 disc. The day after the MRI, I had back surgery. The procedure was called a "microdiscectomy." The surgery was totally painless and the alleviation of my severe suffering was immediate. I spent two nights in the hospital and that was it. Within two weeks I was back playing ugly golf. My golf buddies couldn't believe that I had just undergone surgery. They demanded to see the surgical scar as proof that a procedure had been performed.

After this very short recovery, I decided that I needed to go back to work. It seemed as though that as soon as I had made the decision my phone began to ring off the hook with recruiters calling with job opportunities. I accepted a job offer with a company that was headquartered in New Orleans. The next eighteen months there were magical. Employee turnover which had been over 40 percent suddenly stopped. We were adding customers and employees. Our technology deployed was leading edge and performed well. I started as Vice President of Network Operating and Engineering and, within eighteen months, had become Executive VP of

Network Ops and Engineering, then President and Chief Operating Officer of the company. Our success was talked and written about in various media. We also attracted the attention of Wall Street and then things began to change and not for the better. I knew myself so much better and knew that the company and I had to split. I resigned after eighteen months.

When I resigned after eighteen months from the first start-up company I worked for, I had no idea that another Competitive Local Exchange Carrier (CLEC) across the street would find me. My tenth-floor window faced theirs.

When I negotiated an Interconnection Agreement with SBC Telecom (Southwestern Bell) in their Dallas building, I met with about twenty of their people (fifteen attorneys) on the tenth floor. I was very nervous and felt outnumbered. These were not friendly negotiations. The four SBC buildings in "Bell Plaza" spoke to their awesome power. Two years later SBC hired me as a Director on a $3 billion project. My operations were located on the entire tenth floor of the same building. I could not imagine at that moment that I would be working there in the same building on the same floor.

I love how the complexities of our lives are not so incomprehensible if we listen and pay close attention to our surroundings and our thoughts. Out of my office window in Dallas, I could see the TXU's (Texas Utilities) headquarters building.

CHAPTER 20

MY ULTIMATE TEST OF FAITH
PART I

Getting a yearly physical exam by a doctor was a practice that I had followed for many years. My company had always urged employees to carry out this annual routine. It was a good habit to have even though I had always enjoyed great health except for the bumps and bruises from playing tennis and basketball. The current modern exams give you a computer printout about all of your body's systems and how they are functioning. If something is out of range, then usually further testing or a referral to a specialist is recommended. About thirteen years ago, my primary care doctor noticed that my PSA (prostate specific antigen) test results were very high. They rate the aggressiveness of the cancer with a scale number between 1 and 10. It's called a Gleason score. I tested at a 5. Not good! He referred me to a urology specialist for additional testing.

After my first examination, the urologist recommended a prostate biopsy. This test more definitively determines the absence or presence of cancer. Can you imagine the trepidation I felt? In my fifty-plus years of living, I had only faced one other serious health issue. It was two ruptured discs in my lower back from carrying a heavy tree trunk at age nineteen (later to be aggravated to the point of back surgery from lifting a lawn mower). I have worked and not missed a day for twenty-plus years. I could give a lot of details about the biopsy procedure but it would be too graphic. Guys have a choice of a local anesthetic or to be asleep. I chose to stay awake because it lessens the likelihood of complications due to anesthesia. Prior to my biopsy I had a conversation with a good friend who had recently gone through the same procedure. He mentioned that before his surgery he had gone through three prostate biopsies. I asked him how many core samples had been taken during each biopsy. His response was shocking and a bit scary. He said, "Oh about thirty to forty."

I told this to my urologist before he began and he said, "No, it's only twelve!" After the urologist took five or six samples I lost count. It felt like forty!

Three days after the biopsy I received a telephone call from my doctor. He calmly told me that he had bad news for me. He said, "You have prostate cancer!" This sentence hit me like a baseball bat swung full force into my stomach. It took me a moment to start breathing again. After a short pause the doctor began speaking again. He said that there was some good news. This type of cancer was treatable in most cases when caught in its early stages. He said that I needed to come back to his office in order to review my treatment options. This diagnosis triggered thoughts for me of how truly magical and wonderful my life's journey had been so far. I am satisfied with how I have lived my life. My children are grown up and have their own lives to live. This is not a fatalistic attitude but one of acceptance of my fate and to move forward with a positive approach in dealing with cancer's nasty outcomes. Treatments included radiation, chemo, and radioactive seed implants all having side effects like impotence and incontinence. My doctor told me at a later visit that my chances of a good outcome were fifty-fifty. He said that I needed to do something immediately! This pissed me off. How about a cure outside of surgery? That option was never mentioned.

My thoughts and energy turned to my condition as I read everything that I could find on the subject of prostate cancer. It was amazing how information I needed just kept coming to me. The Law of Attraction was again at work. When we focus our attention on something that comes into our reality, it is truly amazing what new knowledge and information comes to the forefront of our consciousness. I refocused my positive beliefs toward myself and as not having cancer. I refused to even call it by its name aloud. I renewed in my mind my purpose for the rest of my life. I shared my little problem with a few friends and family members. Their support was tremendous. I have since found a wonderful urologist who is the head of the department at his hospital. He and I agree that I should take another biopsy.

Double ouch! This biopsy was, as before, twelve tissue samples ripped from my prostate gland. This time around it felt more like one hundred samples were being taken, not just twelve.

CHAPTER 21

DO THE RIGHT THING

During my many work-careers, there have been many instances where my mental and physical mettle were tested. One particular instance involved one of my most gifted and dedicated supervisors. He had accepted a promotion in Bell Core located in Lisle, Illinois to become an instructor. This was a very desirable job that had direct input from Bell Laboratories. This was also a time when the company had started to change with the implementation of workforce reductions. The rule, at that time, was if you had a viable job offer and you did not accept it you were terminated regardless of your job performance.

Upon further consideration, my supervisor changed his mind about accepting this promotion. The ruling came down hard that either he take the job or be terminated. When this situation came to my attention I knew that this would be a terrible mistake and a great loss of a talented person for our company. I decided to step in and escalated the situation to my tough but fair boss. He would not concede to the logic of keeping our employee at first but after my constant badgering over several days he relented. Through my persistence and my boss's intervention we were able to retain the supervisor in his current position. It was a win-win all around. I reached him by phone that evening and said, "Don't leave, you are staying here with us."

It wasn't until years later that I discovered the reason why my supervisor had first accepted the promotion but then decided to back out of his commitment to move to Lisle, Illinois. Traveling to Lisle today, with the upgrades to the interstate system, would take more than thirteen hours. Thirty years ago, it would have taken longer. The drive would have also been very dangerous because my supervisor's wife was pregnant. Not only was she pregnant but there also were difficulties with the pregnancy. Rather than risk his job my supervisor had packed his car and was about to make the perilous journey when he received my eleventh-hour call to stay.

A few years ago I had the chance to meet my now-close friend's wife. "I never had the opportunity before to say 'thank-you' for what you did for us," she said. When she saw the puzzled look on my face she went on to explain. She said that due to the pregnancy issues they surely would have lost their baby boy during the drive to Lisle. Today that baby boy is a physician in Boston, Massachusetts.

Hurricane Gustav

In 2008 I was working for a video, Internet, and telephone company based in Baton Rouge, Louisiana. Prior to the storm hitting the area, my team began making all the necessary emergency preparations. However, all our preparations could not match the devastation left by the high winds and rain. Even before the storm had passed, the force of the winds had taken its toll on the area and power outages began to mount. While local officials were appearing on television and radio stations cautioning the public to stay off the roadways and be safe, they were verbally beating up our Public Affairs Director because their Emergency Operations Center's (EOC) Internet and video were down. In order to correct the situation, we needed to bring an emergency generator out to the location and mount it on a pole with the node that supplied their building.

I could not ask any of my employees to compromise their safety while I stayed at the office. I called on my supervisor of that area to find me the biggest bucket truck that he could, and I asked if he felt he could safely drive me to the location. He replied that he could. I looked like Big Bird in my oversized yellow rain suit that was brought for me to wear. We drove to the site and was met by another cable technician who had volunteered to help. Despite the wind and rain, we were able to hang the emergency generator and succeeded in getting the EOC back online. To ensure that services were up and running, we went inside the EOC and spoke with the Mayor of Baton Rouge and verified that everything was working. Actions very often speak louder than words.

Doing what you know, in your gut, is right takes strength and empathy that we all have. However, some people in life do not care to exercise it. The more you exercise your human gifts, the stronger they become. The more you examine issues and information from different vantage points, the clearer your decisions and paths become.

CHAPTER 22

IT'S GOING TO RAIN, MAN!

As a very young child growing up I always heard my grandmother and aunts say that I was born with a "veil." Others in the little community I lived in also knew this fact. I recently googled "born with a veil," and the various articles I read were very interesting. Did the fact that others believed I had special gifts convince me too? Did the fact that I spent so much time outside close to nature make me more sensitive to nature? I don't know the definitive answer, but I do know that it has served me and others very well. Decide for yourself after reading the following stories; a mystical veil, a closeness to nature, or possibly both.

While playing in a golf tournament at a course called "The Bluffs" in Louisiana I told my team that we needed to head back to the clubhouse quickly because there was bad weather approaching and would be over the course very soon. The sky was partly cloudy but not at all threatening, so my request was met with skepticism. The group I was playing with consisted of Senior Management/Vice Presidents who are known to be classic type-A personalities. They are often very strong willed, opinionated and not prone to a colleague's sudden weather prediction. Not only did that prediction go against what they could see with their own eyes but also against their desire to continue playing. I told my playing partner to drive me back to the clubhouse immediately, and he could rejoin the team on the next hole. I could sense what my team was thinking, "What a fool."

When we reached the clubhouse, the sky opened up and torrential rain began falling along with dangerous lightning and thunder. All groups who stayed on the course found themselves stranded. From the clubhouse I could see golf carts were scurrying all over the place trying to escape the rain. There was no escape. The rain was coming down sideways and the winds were twenty to thirty miles per hour making umbrellas useless. Eventually everyone made it back to the clubhouse safely but drenched. I greeted the others with a cool drink in my hand, dry clothes and with a "I told you so" smile. I have always had an internal barometer that works to this day.

Katrina

Two weeks before Hurricane Katrina hit New Orleans I told my usual golf buddies that I had a feeling that something very bad was going to happen here concerning the weather. We were playing golf at Lakewood Country Club on the west bank of New Orleans. The three guys I play with are thirty-five- to forty-year friends and co-workers. They are accustomed to hearing such things from me so they listened. Lakewood golf course was destroyed during the storm with over two thousand trees lost. Lakewood has since reopened and it is more beautiful than before that devastating storm.

One of my former bosses would seek my advice when dangerous storms were entering the gulf. Was it going to hit us? If so, what would the impact be on our customers, employees, and our infrastructure? Telephone, Internet, and cellular services are referred to as "lifelines" for a reason. In every case I was correct in my analysis. I have been responsible for those critical services for every hurricane that has come ashore in Louisiana over the last forty-four years.

During one of these hurricane threats our Disaster Planning Group and senior leaders in Atlanta were discussing the probability of being struck in Louisiana. Although Florida had been hit by several hurricanes the year before, the focus was on Louisiana and the fear of another Katrina. When the Big Boss in Atlanta asked for our local team's input, I announced that the storm would go ashore in Florida and not Louisiana. His reply was a contemptuous, "What weather report are you looking at?" My boss gave me a quiet, knowing smile of confidence in my prediction. The storm hit Florida the next day.

<u>Air Quality</u>

One day while conducting a meeting with my human resources staff, the discussion turned to the air quality in our buildings and conference rooms. During the conversation, I mentioned that I could feel when the air quality (too much carbon dioxide) in a room such as the one we were in changed. My Safety and Environmental Manager said, "Bull****! No one can detect that." He said that I have an air quality detection unit at my desk that tested for such changes and that I must be using it. I told him to go get it and bring it back to the conference room. When he returned I said, "Place it under the conference table and I will tell you when it is about to alarm." There were twenty of us in the room and the gauntlet had been thrown down. Everyone was ready to have a good laugh at my expense. We continued with our agenda for about thirty minutes when I suddenly interrupted the meeting and said, "Mike, the air quality is really bad now." He looked at me and ten seconds later the measuring device went into alarm with a loud shrill siren. Mike's eyes got wide and his mouth fell open. Some of the staff applauded and some knowingly smiled. I didn't think anything of it.

<u>Don't Do That!</u>

I have learned not to ignore my inner feelings about many internal or external situations. The week after receiving the great news about being cancer free, I was playing a round of golf on a beautiful sunshiny day. I felt great, and my game was even better. I hit a new ball from the fairway a very long distance away that disappeared into a clump of grass. When I reached where I thought the ball had landed, I noticed that the clump of grass actually marked a drain culvert which meant that I would be able to take a free drop. It was a new ball, so yes, I wanted my free drop! I approached the culvert and caught sight of the ball, "Ah there it is." As I was about to stick my bare hand into the culvert to retrieve the ball, I heard a clear voice in my head say, "David, you grew up here, and you should know better than to stick your hand and arm into a dark recess." I quickly pulled back at that moment and retrieved a long club from my golf bag. When I stuck the club into the opening a five- or six-foot, black, venomous water-moccasin snake struck at my golf club head. I immediately jumped back! I could now see that the snake had wrapped itself around my gold ball. Normally I would have killed that snake in order to retrieve my ball but not today. Today the snake and I were both winners. I turned to my playing partner and said, "The snake can keep that ball."

Once again I had listened to my inner voice and avoided a situation that easily could have been fatal.

CHAPTER 23

MY ULTIMATE TEST OF FAITH PART II

Every December I give thanks to the true meaning of Christmas and count my many blessings. I also use this time to look forward into the coming year. I try to imagine every situation that may come my way both personally and professionally. Through my thoughts, I visualize each possible challenge and how I intend to handle them.

It's January and the holidays are over. My second biopsy was performed by the head of urology at Tulane Medical Center. The results of the tissue analysis would be covered with me on February 10. I listened to my doctor's analysis of the first biopsy, and we both agreed that surgery using the da Vinci robotic system was the best option; still a chance of life-altering complications but the best option for me. It would mean two nights in the hospital and eight to ten days of being attached to a catheter. I figured I would miss, at most, three to five days of work.

Since my commute to and from work is 178 miles round trip I would sometimes stay overnight if there was an early morning or late night function. One day in January such an occasion presented itself. I had a work function that required my presence and knowing it would last late into the evening a hotel reservation was made. That night, a very special and magical night, I was awakened at 3:00 a.m. by what appeared to be a glowing light in my room. I looked around but could not determine where it was coming from. The television wasn't on, and there were no windows in the room. I watched the light with my usual scientific curiosity. Where was this light coming from in my dark hotel room? As the light approached, it became very soft and soothing in appearance. I began to realize how really good I felt. Starting with my head and moving down my body the light seemed to wash over me. When it moved over my abdominal area it stopped and stayed there for several moments. I then heard a voice say in my head, "You no longer have prostate cancer. You are totally healthy. Nothing is wrong with you." I felt great. The next day at work I told a couple of my co-workers about my experience. They have worked with me for close to ten years, and they were not at all surprised by what I relayed to them. I forgot about this event as the work demands of the new year kept me busy.

I have probably learned more about human cell physiology than I ever wanted to know. Mind and body are truly one. I have been working out at the gym fairly regularly. I have been eating good food and taking supplements for prostate health. The first change I noticed was an increase in strength. While playing golf on weekends with some of my lifelong friends, I noticed I could now drive my tee shot about one hundred yards further than a year ago. Par fours that I could never reach in two shots I now can fly the ball over the green on my second shot. People that I bump into at work tell me how fit I look, heavy but fit. I think to myself, "If they only knew what deadly thing was growing inside of me." I caught myself. There is nothing but healthy and goodness inside of me. I refuse to believe otherwise. My golf buddies know my situation and they refuse to accept that anything is wrong with me. They say, "Nothing can kill crab grass." I am the crab grass.

It's February 10, and I am on my way to hear my biopsy results. My appointment is at 1:00 p.m. The doctor's office is very busy, and I am asked to wait in a very small room. An inch of snow had already fallen in New Orleans for the first time in many years. Good omen I thought. My wait is now about an hour. I hear the doctor down the hall consoling a patient and his wife; his news isn't good. I hear the doctor cover the treatment options at least four times. I listen with empathy. I know how bad news feels. I quietly say a prayer for the man. I can feel and understand their pain. Finally the doctor arrives and sits down across from me holding my folder in his hand. Our eyes lock on each other. I feel my body brace for whatever he has to tell me. He opens the folder in a very emphatic powerful way. He flips through the folder of about fifty pages before he begins to go over my results. Finally I think that here is my moment of truth. I have been brave my whole life for others, so now I'll be brave for myself.

He tells me, "Your prostate velocity is a twenty-eight." Okay. "The blood vessels going to your prostate are well dilated," he said.

"What does that mean?" I asked.

"Good blood supply," he replies. "Some cells are articulated." Okay. "You don't have cancer." "Okay but what is my

Gleason score?" It was a six from the first biopsy indicating a moderate to high tumor growth rate. My prostate specific antigen level was a 5.74. For my age 4.0 is considered normal. I am hoping fervently that it is still a six or less. The snow is beginning to come down heavier now, and the telecommunications networks and Internet are crashing due to the heavy load of everyone trying to use them. I tell my doctor that I need to get to work in order to start our emergency recovery plans. "What is my Gleason score?" I ask again and again. Suddenly he hits the desk with his fist. I am startled.

He smiles at me and says, "David, you don't have a Gleason. It's zero. You do not have cancer anymore!" I asked the doctor to explain to me how could that be? His reply was that they had thoroughly examined each cell in the twelve samples and there were no cancer cells anywhere. He said that he could not explain it but when I get home tonight I should get on my knees and thank God. I replied, "I already have." A big smile broke out at the same time on both our faces. We proceeded to discuss for the next ten to fifteen minutes about helping the youth of our area. I told the doctor that I had begun speaking to various students about life, and this good news would allow me to continue to do so for years to come.

The snow in New Orleans turned out to be, after all, a good omen of things to come. Two days later the sun was out, the weather was warm, and I was playing golf with a good friend.

CHAPTER 24

ALWAYS BE GRATEFUL

Growing up enduring many hardships and going through all of life's many challenges I never really thought that anything was very difficult or trying. No matter the trial or tribulation, I always had the perspective that it was just part of growing up. There was a time, at one of my lowest points, I roamed outside between homes and shacks with nowhere to go to get out of the rain. I thought, "It sure would be great to be somewhere dry and warm." This wish led me to the belief that once the rain stopped I would dry out. Rainy walks to school with no umbrella simply meant getting wet and drying out. Then my aunt, who was the epitome of a saint, came along. Although I slept on the floor of her two-room house, lying only on a sheet with another one covering me, I was grateful that I had a roof over my head. There was no thought that I was sleeping on a cold, hard floor; I was grateful to have shelter from the elements.

In the first two years of employment as a telephone technician, I saved every paycheck taking only enough money for lunch and gas. At the end of those two years, I built a house for my aunt. It was a three-bedroom frame house and because Lower Coast Algiers is below sea level it was built on pillars. She never once hinted or asked for a new house nor did I consult or tell her of my plans to build one. I just did it! It felt natural. I felt good that I could give my aunt something back that she always wanted: a three-bedroom home with a separate living room and kitchen. It still stands today even though she passed many years ago due to diabetes complications. It was my fervent wish that she would be there to see me graduate from college. I mentioned this to one of my college professors that I was sitting with at graduation and he said, "She is here and she sees you."

After graduating from high school and after working in the telephone industry I found it so interesting how we can be steered in the right direction in our life's pursuit if we focus and listen to what's going on around us. I now realize that no matter what I'm going through in life it's merely part of the journey and part of the test the universe gives to enable us to grow. Mankind's purpose, I have found, is to grow. If we're listening to anything around us we should seize every day as a learning opportunity to increase our abilities in whatever field we've chosen. I still do this every day. I notice things for the first time every day, and I learn things for the first time every day. If you would only pay attention to your surroundings, it will be the same for you.

If we each as individuals tried to give back something in our skills, abilities, or wealth to others, our great country and people would become even greater. The more we give to each other, the better we become.

CHAPTER 25

LAUGHING AT YOURSELF AND THE IMPORTANCE OF IT

To be open to the many wonderful things that life offers us, we must always remain humble and not take ourselves or things too seriously. A few times during my life I have had my ego get a little too big, and in each instance nature pulled me back to my true purpose. Here are three examples.

I am walking to my office in downtown New Orleans dressed to the max in my blue suit and tie. I am carrying my very fine, new leather briefcase, and it feels good. As I walk I hear loud laughter behind me. There is an old guy bent over double laughing. I look around to see what was so funny. I don't see anyone else or anything funny. The old man gets enough of his composure back to begin talking and points a skinny finger toward me and says, "I see you in your nice suit. I know you are pure country." He's right but how does he know? As I kept walking and thinking I reached up and twisted a piece of sweet straw grass I had broken off and put into my mouth reflexively. It then hit me like a slap in the face. I broke into a spontaneous laugh too. What the old gentleman told me was right and at that moment I remembered who I was and where I had come from.

Another opportunity came in 1990 when I was studying international business at a university in Paris, France. One evening as I was watching television and trying to translate the French I was hearing I thought and felt that I had finally made it. Here I was, half way around the world living in the lap of luxury, if only temporarily, thinking of my friends and family and what they would say if they could see me now. Needless to say that I was feeling satisfied with myself. At that moment, the television program changed to a golf tournament back in the United States. They were showing a shot from the overhead blimp. It was a beautiful highly forested area that was only interrupted by the golf course that had been carved out in one area. I was looking down at my home site where so much of my life had transpired. This was a very humbling moment for me and forever taught me what a small world it really is.

I was chosen by my company to give a presentation to the juniors and seniors at the University of New Orleans. The topic I chose to speak about was what they could expect in the workplace after they graduated and joined the workforce. I had discovered that I had difficulty delivering a speech that had been written by our public affairs group or anyone else for that matter. It had to be my own words. I completed what would be my presentation just in time to make it to the dining area. There were approximately four hundred to six hundred students there in total. I thought in order to make the speech as beneficial to the students as possible I would interject thoughts and experiences from recent college graduates. As I got further into my presentation, I realized that what was meant to be a serious talk about what to expect became hilarious experiences I had. An example was having one of my supervisors tell me that I was working him too hard. It didn't sound funny when I wrote it but it was when I read it out loud. This happened a few more times during the talk. I had a good time laughing at myself during the speech and the audience did too.

When you throttle your ego and unquestioned biases you allow truth to filter through to your mind, and you keep growing as a human being. We are all connected on this planet, galaxy, and universe. I often think that if we remembered this fact there would be less hatred and selfishness in our world.

Scientific research is arriving at new frontiers every day. The pace of change and information available to us is truly amazing, but we must keep our humanity at the forefront of our existence. This hectic pace of change right now can really knock you off balance in life. Stay grounded and laugh a little, no laugh a lot.

CHAPTER 26

TEACHERS AND MENTORS

Teachers

Teachers have always played a critical role in my development as a person all the way from elementary school through college. My elementary school teachers saw something in me worth developing, and I was elected to perform in various school plays from first grade through sixth grade. I was also in the school choir and helped in many extracurricular activities. I now realize that they were helping me overcome my extreme shyness and being an introvert. Some years after college I bumped into my fourth grade teacher?"

He said, "Of course I do, David. You were the kid who knew the answers to all my questions." That comment made me smile, but it also made me realize that I had thought of myself in that way.

My high-school teachers were very inspirational to me. They each took an interest in what and how I was doing in school. Knowing that I was walking fourteen miles every day to and from school, some of the teachers tried pooling their money to buy me a car. It would be years later before

I discovered what they had been willing to do for me. One of the high-school assistant counselors told me that he had written his graduate research paper using me as his case study. He never let me read it but I remember asking him, "Is it about how I keep dropping out of school and coming back in and acing all my exams?"

He smiled and replied, "Yes."

When the crops, on the farms where I and others worked, were ready for harvesting we would all drop out of school to work the fields. My high-school counselor would drive to my home and drive me into school in order to reinstate me.

College was the same story. My professors became very interested and involved in who I was. I loved every course and put forth my best effort into whatever class I was taking. When my work schedules would interfere with classes or exams, they would flexibly work with me to help solve my conflicts. In return I have given my time and efforts to help educators, both in schools and universities, in any way they see there is a need. Whether it's mentoring students, giving speeches, or motivational speeches I am grateful for the opportunity to give back to those who have inspired me.

We as a nation do not honor enough the people who touch the minds and souls of our youth.

<u>Mentors</u>

For a very long time I believed that everything I did to become successful and self-sufficient in my life was accomplished solely by me. Whereas I did survive a tremendous amount of physical and mental hardships alone, looking back, I now realize that there were people who were there for me to give me a nudge or advice to push me in the right direction. I could not have made it through many situations without their insight and wisdom. The term mentor (advisor, counselor, guru, confidante, etc.) did not even exist in our nomenclature back then. The "angels" seemed to just materialize in my life at the moment that I needed their guidance.

School Counselor

Earlier I mentioned that my high-school counselor would drive the long distance to my home just to pick me up and bring me back to school. He did this many times throughout my high-school years. During one of the drives back to school, I remember him telling me that with my intelligence, if I would just stay in high school and graduate, I would be successful in life. He also said that due to my intelligence I would never really fit in but must stay true to my own beliefs.

Joe

During my work-career there were many guiding lights for me. When I entered the ranks of management at the tender age of twenty-three years, I replaced a supervisor who moved to a new position in the same building in downtown New Orleans. During this time period, there were hundreds of employees in this complex and the management team must have numbered in the twenties. It was still a very rare occurrence to see a person of my hue in management. The senior supervisors would always give me the crappy assignments and would make discriminatory comments just loud enough for me to hear. I would, however, continue to focus on whatever job I had and on the people who reported to me. Some others would make snide comments about me working and going to college. I endured it but not easily. There was a particularly spiteful supervisor who was always nasty to everyone and especially to me. One evening he just got me so angry that I had had enough and I was ready to physically go after him. It seemed like Joe appeared out of nowhere in the office and said, "Come take a walk with me to the patio and smoke a cigarette." I went with him and he gave me a cigarette, a Camel brand, which was very strong. I started coughing, choking and my eyes began to water. I had never smoked! Joe began to laugh so hard and so did I. He calmed me down and said that all the negative comments and insults were just a case of jealously. The next week or so we had our monthly managers' meeting with the entire team. Joe stood up in the meeting and began to address the group. He said, "You all need to leave this man alone. He will be our boss one day." Everyone got quiet.

I thought to myself, "What is he talking about?" His declaration, however, did work. The harassment stopped. Some years later, I reflected back on Joe's comment. I had been promoted several times and everyone in Central Office Operations reported to me, including Joe. I told him how much I had learned from his temperament and how much I appreciated his guidance. I asked him how he knew ahead of time what my career path would be. He said that he just could see it in me. This is just one of several people who have had a positive impact on my life and who I am.

<u>Margaret</u>

Mentors or guiding lights appear throughout our lives. Again, it is very important to be aware of this and to be aware of the messaging and valuable knowledge that is being proffered. William Shakespeare wrote in *Julius Caesar*, "…for the eye sees not itself, but by reflection, by some other things." The meaning that I take from this quote is that we cannot see ourselves but by how people reflect who we are. Another significant mentor in my work life was a woman district manager who was my boss's boss. Margaret had a reputation for being tough but fair. She had to be very tough and brilliant to advance in the male-dominated culture that we worked in. She gave me different assignments that she knew were out of my comfort zone which knocked me off balance for a while but always turned out as preparation for a future that I could not see. She promoted me from supervisor to manager and set the groundwork for me to become a senior director of the company. There was so much inner strength within her; strength which was needed to survive and thrive in that male-dominated management system.

Her insight and trust in me came through one day when she transferred me to a completely different electronic switching computer system. I was stunned. The complexity of the hardware and software that required years of study and training to understand and manage was now mine. This change in job assignment, to a totally different operating system, reduced my knowledge to almost zero. I dove into the new assignment and worked day and night to get up to speed. Soon thereafter another new technology came out of Bell Laboratories: digital switching. The technology I was now managing was a stepping stone to the new stuff. She knew this was a great path for me and it turned out that she was exactly right. Margaret is still a guiding light to me. We are still friends and communicate to this day.

Sal

Another mentor in my career died in 2013, but he still comes to my mind often and sometimes in my dreams at night. His official position in my organization was that of staff manager but, in reality, his job was to eliminate roadblocks and problems in the organization. After he retired from the company where we had met, Sal lent his knowledge and talents to me in three other companies that I ran. He worked and continued to help me until the last four days of his life. I knew that he was seriously ill but not that his passage was imminent. Such was his strength of character and his wonderful sense of humor. I still have several of his e-mails to me in my inbox because I cherish his many words of wisdom to me. We loved working together and tackling problems that were deemed impossible. They never were impossible to us. One of his favorite sayings was, "We thrive on adversity." We did just that and learned from the experience.

In my staff meetings we covered many complex issues and problems that had never arisen before due to the new technology that was coming online fast and furious. Sal would take the discussion we had and turn them into an action plan that we would follow. He had the gift and ability to turn my thoughts and words into something tangible and actionable.

Sal was a Vietnam-War veteran and during his tour there was exposed times to Agent Orange chemicals. Later in life he developed the health ailments that went along with this exposure. The military denied his disability requests several times over the years. We would look at each rejection, review his documents, and resubmit proof of his military service. He eventually won his case.

Adversity, persistence, reward.

CHAPTER 27

JOBS

Farm Hand

I started working as a farm hand in the fields of Plaquemine parish as a ten-year-old and continued off and on until I was fifteen. I worked side by side with many of my relatives planting crops such as tomatoes, mustard greens, squash, and turnips and then harvesting them when matured. The work was from sunup to sundown in the cold weather of fall and winter and again in the heat of spring and summer. The work was continuous with no time for rest periods. If hungry, lunch would be eating whatever crop was in season. If it was tomato season I would just simply pick the ripe Creoles, wipe off the Sevin dust, and eat a few. This was backbreaking work for pay of only two or three dollars a day, but it was honest work.

I learned patience while doing this painstakingly slow work. To this day, I still use the knowledge I learned of seasonal planting and harvesting in my own vegetable garden.

Auto Mechanic

I took this job the summer after graduating from high school. I had always worked on our family's cars, as they often broke down, so I already had the skills to perform tune ups, changing brake shoes, changing transmissions, etc. During this time I was still working at the State School from 11:00 p.m. until 7:00 a.m. I kept this job until it was time for me to start college. Although the pay was good in this job it didn't satisfy an internal need or desire for something more. I wanted to move on.

<u>Gretna Glass Works—Shop Mechanic</u>

This was my first job I had after leaving college in Baton Rouge. I had never worked in this industry before, and I learned a lot about handling glass and mirrors. I was the only shop assistant to the master glass cutters and installers. I kept busy all day assisting anyone in the shop who needed help. After a few weeks, one of the two company owners came over to me and asked me to stop working for a few minutes to talk to him. He was very pleased with my work and wanted to know more about me. I told him about my background and how I had just left college in Baton Rouge. I explained that my money had run out and that I realized that architectural engineering was not where my heart was. My great passion was science, and in particular, physics. He looked me directly in the eyes and said, "We like your work here, but you are insulting your intelligence with this menial work. You should go back to college." I resigned the next week.

<u>Telecommunication Technician</u>

This was my entry-level job and entry into the world of telecommunications. I performed this job for about three years before I was promoted into management. After several months on the job, my boss decided to put me on the 4:00 p.m. to midnight shift, so that I could go back to college. I was able to perform all my work functions and still have a little time to study. Being alone most of the time on the four to midnight shift allowed me to delve into various operations more deeply and learn to problem solve many situations on my own.

Working alone one night I had the task of modifying several dial pulse circuits (rotary dial) to the new touchtone (push button) circuits. The lights and power suddenly went off in the frame room where I worked. The long frame walkway, approximately one hundred feet, was totally dark without the overhead lights and the soldering irons on each ladder went cold. I thought, "Oh No! These customers will be irritated to have to wait additional days for their touchtone phone service." I found an electrical extension cord that was long enough to let me reach the length of the frame from one essential outlet where the red "exit" lamp was. I used it to heat up one soldering iron. I had a pen flashlight in my toolkit and I used the light from that small source in order to complete the wiring and make the connection.

The following Monday when my boss saw me he was very apologetic for his failure to tell me that the whole building would be shut down for much-needed power work. He said that we will just change the due dates on the touchtone orders and complete the wiring changes later in the week. I smiled at him and said, "Boss, no need to do that. The wiring was completed."

He asked, "How could you do that work with no lights or electrical power?"

I told him about the extension that I used to the soldering iron and that I held my flashlight in my mouth so that I could see. Doing so allowed me to hold the solder in one hand and the soldering iron in the other. He said that anyone else would have given up. I never give up.

Supervisor—Frame Operations in the Downtown New Orleans Switching Complex

This was my first foray in a managerial position. I had ten direct reports all of whom were older than me. Every day my crew would run the wiring for new and existing customer telephone service. Our workday was dependent upon how many service orders came in. This position gave me my initial look into the nature of people and how they acted and reacted to different situations. I also learned that I had an innate ability to listen, find common ground, and connect to others very easily.

Electronic Switching Systems Supervisor

This was a new method of connecting and switching telephone calls and circuitry created by Bell Laboratories. This job consisted of handling one of the newest and most complex computer systems in the world. The operating system was named "Duplex Multi-Environment Real Time Operating System." What a ridiculous name for an operating system!

Switching Control Center Supervisor

I was involved in central control and maintenance of several electronic switching systems in several different cities. The Switching Control Center (SCC) allowed technicians to observe and react to problems occurring in real time. Because both the hardware and software were brand new so were the problems that arose. This was a very exhilarating time.

Manager—Central Office Operations and Switching Control Centers

Operation of the Switching Systems (computers) which included surveillance and investigation of alarms and all programming functions was now under my leadership. Before moving to the next level of management, I had responsibility of approximately two hundred employees.

District Manager—Central Office Operations

This is the third level of management (supervisor, manager, district manager), which carried the responsibility for all communications in the New Orleans area. The functions of this position mirrored that of the manager except now I was the department head overall of the switching systems and centers in the southern region of Louisiana.

Senior Director Human Resources—Louisiana

I was responsible for all personnel functions in Louisiana reporting directly to HR Headquarter in Atlanta, Georgia. As mentioned in chapter 16, the responsibilities included but not limited to handling affirmative action initiative, discrimination charges against the company, employee pay benefits, training initiatives for employees, and environmental hazards mitigation. This job taught me very quickly how problems can grow into something nuclear if they are allowed to fester and not handled when the issue first arises.

Senior Director—Operational Centers and Field Functions

My responsibilities for this job included all the data and control centers that received customer repair requests as well as installations for new service. It also included the engineering planning and construction of new service areas (residential neighborhoods and businesses) for new copper cable, fiber optic cable, and the supporting electronics (nodes). I learned that the broad scope and responsibilities of this job made me more dependent on my workforce. I learned how much people can grow and achieve if management trusts them to do their jobs.

Vice President—Network Planning, Engineering, and Field Operations

This position was at a new Competitive Local Exchange Company (CLEC). This was the term coined by the Federal Communications Commission for brand-new telephone companies which were now legally allowed to become a telephone provider.

I was given the task to literally build the infrastructure of both people and equipment into a successful telephone and Internet-service provider. One unfortunate and painful lesson I learned was that there are evil, greedy, and unethical people in some businesses. Our early success attracted the sharks from venture capital groups whose sole motivation was to take over the company and they did.

President and Chief Operating Officer

This job was also at a Competitive Local Exchange Company. I was again responsible for building the company's infrastructure; however, with a new title came new responsibilities. More control in the decision-making process led to endless hours in meetings—meetings to review and select equipment vendors; meetings to review and sign contracts; and meetings with our lawyers. Once again, our success drew the venture capital groups and in the end the company was merged with another out-of-state company.

Vice President and Chief Technology Officer
This position was with a privately owned Rural Independent Local Exchange Carrier (ILEC). I was responsible for all facets of the operations, maintenance, and expansion of telephone, Internet and data. After of years of success, the company decided to downsize and restructure. Surprised by the move, I resigned.

Director/Vice President of Technical Operations
My responsibilities included the daily management for all telephone, Internet, data, and video operations in the Baton Rouge and Lafayette area. I led the successful implementation of telephone services from zero to sixty thousand customers in just three years. I also led projects such as increasing Internet speeds to customers, high-definition TV, and caller ID to the TV.

All the jobs and positions I've described helped to develop the person I am today. Each was a learning experience.

EPILOGUE

Inspiration

Each of the following men have had a profound effect on my thinking and life. They are listed in the order that I met them. All three of these outstanding men are now deceased, but they lived long and fruitful lives. Their body of work will continue to live on and help those who seek their counsel.

William Deming (10/14/1900–12/20/1993)

Dr. Deming has been described as the father of the quality process improvement initiatives in Japan and the United States. The first time I saw Dr. Deming in person was during one of his seminars in New Orleans. The seminar was also broadcast over video to over forty other locations around the country. He is famously known for his book, *Out of the Crisis.* The fourteen points presented by him has changed many companies for the better making them more employee and customer focused.

During a question-and-answer session, Dr. Deming fielded a question from an attendee who asked if he had ever been cheated by one of his PhD candidates by not doing the required course work. Dr. Deming had said that he started all of his students with an "A" to drive out fear. The gentleman rephrased his question again and again in his relentless pursuit to compel Dr. Deming to admit that some student must have cheated him. After a long pause and in the silence of the auditorium, Dr. Deming said, "And who did he cheat?" Dr. Deming had an uncanny ability to reduce the most complex situations to something powerful and straightforward.

Here are two of my favorite quotes from Dr. Deming:

It is not necessary to change. Survival is not mandatory.

There is no substitute for knowledge.

<u>Stephen R. Covey (10/24/1932–7/16/2013)</u>

I had the great fortune of meeting Dr. Covey during two of his seminars. He would stroll through the audience and ask the most profound questions that really made you think about who you are. I recommend his book, *The 7 Habits of Highly Effective People* to every class of students or employees that I have given lectures to or mentored over the past decade. This book has sold over twenty-five million copies since it was written. There is no "end" point in pursuing and gaining knowledge. This is a quest to be made every day.

Here are two Stephen R. Covey quotes:

Leadership is communicating others' worth and potential clearly that they are inspired to see it in themselves.

I am not a product of my circumstances. I am a product of my decisions.

Zygmunt Nagorsky (9/27/1912–6/26/2011)

I met Dr. Zygmunt in a training leadership class entitled "Achieving Peak Performance." I will always remember his penetrating eyes that seemed to look directly into your soul. This class was comprised of about twenty leaders from various disciplines. There were educators, politicians, corporate managers, and others mixed in our grouping. As we met that first morning, Dr. Zygmunt went around the classroom and looked deeply into the eyes of each person. After a few seconds of this he would tell each person what profession they were in. He was uncannily right every time until he got to me. He said, "David, you are an educator." I said, "Nope a corporate leader but I like to think of myself as an educator." I always took the time, energy, and money to ensure that my teams had the best training available. I learned from Dr. Zygmunt that there are not always easy answers to challenges in life but there are answers if we focus hard enough and invest the mental energy to do an in-depth analysis.

As you reflect on where you are in your life look at your closest associates. Are they reflective of your goals and dreams? Are they adding to your life in a positive way? If they are not, seek new friends.

CPSIA information can be obtained
at www.ICGtesting.com
Printed in the USA
LVOW10s0922250617
539310LV00012B/438/P

9 781540 770493